MW00344668

IBN 'ARABI

"*Whoso Knoweth Himself . . .*"

from the

Treatise on Being
(Risale-t-ul-wujudiyyah)

Translation of an Arabic Manuscript in the Hunterian Collection,
Glasgow University by T H WEIR BD (Assistant to the Professor
of Hebrew and Semitic Languages in the University of Glasgow)

BESHARA PUBLICATIONS

© Beshara Design Centre Ltd 1976
Published by Beshara Publications
Hope (Sufferance) Wharf Rotherhithe London SE16
ISBN 0 904975 06 1
Printed by Ithaca Press London SE1

This translation has been published with the full
collaboration and support of
The Muhyiddin Ibn 'Arabi Society

The Saying of the most Great Shaikh Muhyi al Din 'Arabi—may God sanctify his mighty Secret—in Explanation of the saying of him (upon whom be peace): "Whoso knoweth himself knoweth his Lord."

The Kitabu'l Ajwibah—and it is also called the Kitabu'l Alif—by the learned Imâm, the Strong One of the Age, the most Great Shaikh Muhyi al Din Abu 'Abdallah Muhammadi ibn 'Ali, Ibn 'Arabi, al Ta'i, al Hatimi, al Andalusi—may God sanctify his mighty Secret.

In the name of God, the Merciful, the Compassionate, and Him we ask for aid: Praise be to God before whose oneness there was not a before, unless the Before were He, and after whose singleness there is not an after, except the After be He. He is, and there is with Him no after nor before, nor above nor below, nor far nor near, nor union nor division, nor how nor where nor when, nor times nor moment nor age, nor being nor place. And He is now as He was. He is the One without oneness, and the Single without singleness. He is not composed of name and named, for His name is He and His named is He. So there is no name other than He, nor named. And so He is the Name and the Named. He is the First without firstness, and the Last without lastness. He is the Outward without outwardness, and the Inward without inwardness. I mean that He is the very existence of the First and the very existence of the Last, and the very existence of the Outward and the very existence of the Inward.[1] So that there is no first nor last, nor outward nor inward, except Him, without these becoming Him or His becoming them.[2]

Understand, therefore, in order that thou mayest not fall into the error of the Hululis[3]:—He is not in a thing nor a thing in Him, whether entering in or proceeding forth. It is necessary that thou know Him after this fashion, not by knowledge (*'ilm*), nor

---

[1] The Arabic is اعني انه هو وجود حروف الاول الخ .

[2] . بلا صيران هذه الاحرف وجوده الخ

[3] Who believe in incarnations of God.

3

by intellect, nor by understanding, nor by imagination, nor by sense, nor by the outward eye, nor by the inward eye, nor by perception. There does not see Him, save Himself; nor perceive Him, save Himself. By Himself He sees Himself, and by Himself He knows Himself. None sees Him other than He, and none perceives Him other than He. His Veil[4] is [only a part of] His oneness; nothing veils other than He. His veil is [only] the concealment of His existence in His oneness, without any quality. None sees Him other than He—no sent prophet, nor saint made perfect, nor angel brought nigh[5] knows Him. His Prophet is He, and His sending is He, and His word is He. He sent Himself with Himself to Himself. There was no mediator nor any means other than He. There is no difference between the Sender and the thing sent, and the person sent and the person to whom he is sent. The very existence of the prophetic message is His existence.[6] There is no other, and there is no existence to other, than He, nor to its ceasing to be *(fana')*, nor to its name, nor to its named.

And for this the Prophet (upon whom be peace) said: "Whoso knoweth himself knoweth his Lord." And he said (upon him be peace): "I know my Lord by my Lord." The Prophet (upon whom be peace) points out by that, that thou art not thou: thou art

[4] That is, phenomenal existence.
[5] Koran, IV, 170, وَلاَ الْمَلاَئِكَةُ الْمُقَرَّبُونَ..
[6] وجود حروف النبأ وجوده .

He, without thou; not He entering into thee, nor thou entering into Him, nor He proceeding forth from thee, nor thou proceeding forth from Him. And it is not meant by that, that thou art aught that exists or thine attributes aught that exists, but it is meant by it that thou never wast nor wilt be, whether by thyself or through Him or in Him or along with Him. Thou art neither ceasing to be nor still existing. *Thou art He*, without one of these limitations. Then if thou know thine existence thus, then thou knowest God; and if not, then not.

And most of 'those who know God' *(al 'urraf)* make a ceasing of existence and the ceasing of that ceasing a condition of attaining the knowledge of God, and that is an error and a clear oversight. For the knowledge of God does not presuppose the ceasing of existence nor the ceasing of that ceasing. For things have no existence, and what does not exist cannot cease to exist. For the ceasing to be implies the positing of existence, and that is polytheism. Then if thou know thyself without existence or ceasing to be, then thou knowest God; and if not, then not.

And in making the knowledge of God conditional upon the ceasing of existence and the ceasing of that ceasing, there is involved an assertion of polytheism. For the Prophet (upon whom be peace) said, "Whoso knoweth himself," and did not say, "Whoso maketh himself to cease to be." For the affirmation

5

of the other makes its extinction impossible, and [on the other hand] that of which the affirmation is not allowable its extinction is not allowable. Thine existence is nothing, and nothing cannot be added to something, whether it be perishing or unperishing, or existent or non-existent. The Prophet points to the fact that thou art non-existent now as thou wast non-existent before the Creation. For now is past eternity and now is future eternity, and now is past time. And God (whose name be exalted) is the existence of past eternity and the existence of future eternity and the existence of past time, yet without past eternity or future eternity or past time ever existing. For if it were not so He would not be by Himself without any partner, and it is indispensable that He should be by Himself without any partner. For His 'partner' would be he whose existence was in his own essence, not in the existence of God, and whoever should be in that position would not be dependent upon Him. Then, in that case, there would be a second Lord, which is absurd: God (whose name be exalted) can have no partner nor like nor equal. And whoever looks upon anything as being along with God or apart from God or in God, but subject to Him in respect of His divinity, makes this thing also a partner, [only] subject to God in respect of divinity. And whoever allows that anything exists side by side with God, whether self-subsisting or subsisting in Him or capable of ceasing to exist or of ceasing to cease to exist, he is far from what smells of a breath of the knowledge of the soul.

6

Because, whoever allows that he is existent beside God, subsisting in Him, then in Him becoming extinct, and his extinction becoming extinct, then one extinction is linked to another, and that is polytheism upon polytheism. So he is a polytheist, not one who knows God and himself.

Then if one say: How lies the way to the knowledge of the soul and the knowledge of God (whose name be exalted)?—

Then the Answer is: The way of the knowledge of these two is, that thou understand that God is, and that there is not with Him a thing. He is now as He was.

Then if one say: I see myself to be other than God and I do not see God to be myself,—

Then the Answer is: The Prophet (may God bless him and give him peace) meant by the soul thine existence and thy reality, not the 'soul' which is named 'commanding,' 'upbraiding,' and 'pacified';[7] but in the 'soul' he pointed to all that is beside God (whose name be exalted), as the Prophet (may God bless him and give him peace) said: "O my God, show me things as they are clearly," meaning by

[7] For 'soul' here we would say 'flesh'; see Mr. Gibb's "Ottoman Poetry," p. 198.

'things' whatever is beside God (whose name be exalted), that is, "Make me to know what is beside Thee in order that I may understand and know things, which they are—whether they are Thou or other than Thou, and whether they are of old, abiding, or recent and perishing." Then God showed him what was beside Himself, without the existence of what is beside Himself. So he saw things as they are: I mean, he saw things to be the essence of God (whose name be exalted) without how or where. And the name 'things' includes the soul and other than it of things. For the existence of the soul and the existence of other things are both equal in point of being 'things,' that is, are nothing; for, in reality, the thing is God and God is named a thing. Then when thou knowest the things thou knowest the soul, and when thou knowest the soul thou knowest the Lord. Because he whom thou thinkest to be beside God, he is not beside God; but thou dost not know Him, and thou seest Him and dost not understand that thou seest Him. And when this secret is revealed to thee thou understandest that thou art not what is beside God, and that thou art thine own end and thine own object in thy search after thy Lord, and that thou dost not require to cease to be, and that thou hast continued and wilt continue without when and without times, as we mentioned above. And thou seest all thine actions to be His actions, and all His attributes to be thine attributes. Thou seest thine outward to be His outward and thine inward to be His inward, and thy first to be His

8

first and thy last to be His last, without doubting and without wavering. And thou seest thine attributes to be His attributes and thine essence to be His essence, without thy becoming Him or His becoming thee, either in the greatest or least degree. "Everything is perishing except His Face";[8] that is, there is no existent but He, nor existence to other than He, so that it should require to perish and His Face remain; that is, there is nothing except His Face: "then, whithersoever ye turn, there is the Face of God."[9]

It is as if one did not know a thing and afterwards knows it. His existence does not cease, but his ignorance ceases, and his existence continues as it was, without his existence being exchanged for another existence, or the existence of the not-knowing person being compounded with the exist-ence of the knowing, or intermixing, but [merely] a taking away of ignorance. Therefore, think not that thou requirest to cease to be. For if thou requiredst to cease to be, then thou wouldest in that case be His veil, and the veil other than God (whose name be exalted); which requires that another than He should have overcome Him in preventing His being seen; and this is an error and an oversight. And we have mentioned above that His veil is [only a part of] His oneness, and His singleness is not other than it. And, thus it is permitted to him who

[8] Koran XXVIII, 88.
[9] II, 109.

is united to Reality to say, "I am the Truth," and to say, "Praise be to Me." But none attains to union except he see his own attributes to be the attributes of God (whose name be exalted), and his own essence to be the essence of God (whose name be exalted), without his attributes or essence entering into God or proceeding forth from Him at all, or ceasing from God or remaining in Him. And he sees himself as never having been, not as having been and then having ceased to be. For there is no soul save His soul, and there is no existence save His existence.

And to this the Prophet (upon whom be peace) pointed when he said: "Revile not the world, for God—He is the world," pointing to the fact that the existence of the world is God's existence without partner or like or equal. And it is related from the Prophet (upon whom be peace) that he said that God (whose name be exalted) said[10]:

"O my servant, I was sick and thou visitedst Me not, I begged of thee and thou gavest not to Me," with other like expressions; pointing to the fact that the existence of the beggar is His existence, and that the existence of the sick is His existence. And when it is allowed that the existence of the beggar and the existence of the sick are His existence, it is allowed that thy existence is His existence, and that the existence of all created things, both accidents and

[10] To Moses.

10

substances, is His existence. And when the secret of an atom of the atoms is clear, the secret of all created things, both external and internal, is clear, and thou dost not see in this world or the next aught beside God, but the existence of these two Abodes, and their name and their named, all of them, are He, without doubt and without wavering. And thou dost not see God as having ever created anything, but thou seest "every day He is in a business,"[11] in the way of revealing His existence or concealing it, without any quality, because He is the First and the Last and the Outward and the Inward. He is outward in His oneness and inward in His singleness: He is the first in His essence and His immutability, and the last in His everlastingness. The very existence of the first is He, and the very existence of the last is He, and the very existence of the outward is He, and the very existence of the inward is He.[12] He is His name and He is His named. And as His existence is 'necessary,' so the non-existence of all beside Him is necessary. For that which thou thinkest to be beside Him is not beside Him. For He will not have aught to be other than He. Nay, the other is He, and there is no otherness. The other is with His existence and in His existence, outwardly and inwardly.

The person to whom this description is applicable is endowed with many qualities without limit or end.

[11] Koran, LV, 29.
[12] Arabic as on p. 3.

But just as he who dies the death of the body[13] loses all his qualities, both praiseworthy and blameworthy, so in the Sufi death[14] all the qualities, both blameworthy and praiseworthy, are cut off, and God (whose name be exalted) comes into his place in all his states. Thus, instead of his essence comes the essence of God (whose name be exalted), and in place of his attributes come the attributes of God (whose name be exalted).

And so the Prophet (may God bless him and give him peace) said, "Die before ye die," that is, know yourselves before ye die. And he (upon whom be peace) said: "God (whose name be exalted) has said: The worshipper does not cease to draw near to Me with good works until I love him. Then, when I love him, I am to him hearing and sight and tongue and hand unto the end," pointing to the fact that he who knows himself sees his whole existence to be His existence, and does not see any change take place in his own essence or attributes, seeing that he was not the existence of his essence, but was merely ignorant of the knowledge of himself. For when thou 'knowest thyself,' thine egoism is taken away, and thou knowest that thou art not other than God. For, if thou hadst had an independent existence, so that thou didst not require to cease to be or to 'know thyself,' then thou wouldest be a Lord beside Him; and God forbid that He should have created a Lord

13 من مات بصورته
14 الموت المعنوي .

12

beside Himself.

The profit of the knowledge of the soul is, that thou understandest and art sure that thy existence is neither existent nor non-existent, and that thou art not, wast not, and never wilt be.

From this the meaning of the saying, "There is no god but God," is clear, since there is no god other than He nor existence to other than Him, so that there is no other beside Him—and no god but He.

Then if one say: Thou makest void His sovereignty,—

Then the Answer is: I do not make void His sovereignty. For He is still Ruler as well as ruled, and is still Creator as well as created. He is now as He was as to His creative power and as to His sovereignty, not requiring a creature nor a subject, because He is the Creator and the created, and the Ruler and the ruled. When He called into being the things that are, He was [already] endowed with all attributes. And He is now as He was then. In His oneness there is no difference between what is recent and what is original. The recent is the result of His manifesting Himself, and the original is the result of His remaining within Himself. His outward is His inward, and His inward is His outward: His first is His last and His last is His first; and all is one, and the One is all. The definition of Him was, "Every day He is in a business," and there was nothing beside Him, and He is now as He was then, and there is in reality no existence to what is beside Him. As He was in past eternity and past time "every day engaged in a business," and there was no existent thing beside Him, so He is the same now as He was, "every day engaged in a business," and there is no business and there is no day, as there were in past eternity and past time no business and no day. And the existence of the created things and their non-existence are the same thing. And, if it were not so, there would of necessity be an origination of something fresh which was not [before] in His oneness, and that would be a defect, and His oneness is too sublime for that!

Therefore, when thou knowest thyself after this fashion, without adding a like or an equal or a partner to God (whose name be exalted), then thou knowest it as it really is. And it was thus he said (upon whom be peace), "Whoso knoweth himself knoweth his Lord." He did not say, "Whoso maketh himself to cease to be, knoweth his Lord," for he (upon him be peace) understood and saw that there is nothing beside Him. Thereupon he pointed out that the knowledge of the soul was the knowledge of God (whose name be exalted). That is, "Know that thy existence is not thy existence nor other than thy existence. For thou art not existent nor non-existent, nor other than existent nor other than

14

non-existent. Thy existence and thy non-existence are His existence, and yet without there being any existence or non-existence, because thy existence and thy non-existence are actually His existence." So if thou seest things (without seeing another thing along with God) to be Him, thou knowest thyself; and, verily, to know thyself after this fashion is to know God, without wavering and without doubt, and without compounding anything of what is of recent origin with what is original, in any way.

Then if one ask: How lies the way to union, when thou affirmest that there is no other beside Him, and a thing cannot be united to itself?—

Then the Answer is: No doubt there is in reality no union nor division, nor far nor near. For union is not possible except between two, and if there be but one, there can be no union nor division. For union requires two either similar or dissimilar. Then if they are similar they are equals, and if they are dissimilar they are opposites, and He (whose name be exalted) spurns to have either an equal or an opposite; so that the union is something else than union, and the nearness something else than nearness, and the farness something else than farness. So there is union without union, and nearness without nearness, and farness without farness.

Then if anyone say: Explain to us this 'union without union'; and what is the meaning of this 'nearness without nearness' and this 'farness without farness'?—

Then the Answer is: I mean that thou, in thy stages of drawing nigh and of being far off, wast not a thing beside God (whose name be exalted), but thou hadst not the 'knowledge of the soul,' and didst not understand that thou art He without thou. Then when thou art united to God (whose name be exalted)—that is, when thou knowest thyself (although the knowledge itself does not exist[15])--thou understandest that thou art He. And thou wast not aware before that thou wast He, or He other than He. Then, when the knowledge comes upon thee, thou understandest that thou knowest God by God, not by thyself.

To take an example: Suppose that thou dost not know that thy name is Mahmud, or thy named Mahmud. Then if the name and the named be in reality one, and thou thinkest that thy name is Muhammad, and after some time comest to know that thou art Mahmud, then thy existence goes on, but the name Muhammad is cut off from thee, by thy coming to know thyself, that thou art Mahmud, and wast Muhammad only by ceasing to be thyself. And 'ceasing to be' presupposes an affirmation of existence, and whoever posits an existence beside

١٥ اي عرفت نفسك بلا وجود حروف العرفان .

16

Him makes a partner to Him (exalted and blessed be His name). So nothing positive is taken away from Mahmud, nor does Muhammad cease to be in Mahmud, or enter into him or proceed forth from him, nor Mahmud into Muhammad; but as soon as Mahmud knows himself, that he is Mahmud and not Muhammad, he knows himself by himself, not by Muhammad. For Muhammad never existed at all, then how could anything that does exist be known through him?

So, then, the knower and that which he knows are both one, and he who unites and that with which he unites are one, and seer and seen are one. For the knower is His attribute and the known is His essence; and he who unites is His attribute, and that with which he unites is His essence; and the attribute and that to which it is attributed are one. And this is the explanation of the saying "Whoso knoweth himself knoweth his Lord."

So whoever understands this example knows that there is no union nor division, and he knows that the knower is He and the known is He, and the seer is He and the seen is He, he who unites is He and that with which he unites is He. There does not unite with Him other than He, and there is not separated from Him other than He. And whoever understands this is free from the polytheism of polytheism, and, if not, then he has not felt a breath of freedom from polytheism.

Most of 'those who know' (who think that they know themselves and know their Lord, and that they are free from the delusion of existence) say that the Path is not to be traversed except by ceasing to be, and the ceasing of that ceasing. And that is due to their not understanding the saying of the Prophet (may God bless him and give him peace). And because they must blot out polytheism, they point at one time to the negation, that is, the cessation, of existence, and at another to the cessation of that cessation, and at another to effacement, and at another to annihilation. And all these explanations are unadulterated polytheism. For whoever allows that there is anything beside Him, and that afterwards it ceases to be, or allows a cessation of its extinction, he affirms the existence of something that is beside Him, and whoever does this makes a partner to God. May God guide them and us to the middle of the Path!

HYMN

Thou thoughtest, a-thinking, that thou wast thou,
And thou art not thou and never wast thou.
For if thou wert thou, then wert thou a Lord
And a Second of Two. Leave what thou art
    thinking.
There is no difference between the beings of Him
    and Thee:
He is not distinct from thee nor Thou from Him.
For if thou say, in ignorance, that thou art Another,
Thou art stubborn, and if thine ignorance cease,
    thou art docile.
Thy union is flight and thy flight is union,
And thy far is near. In this thou art blessed.
Leave intellect and understand through intuition,
Lest that pass thee by against which thou art
    guarding.
And make no partner to God of anything at all,
In order that it may be well with thee: in polytheism
    thou wast at ease.

Then if one say: Thou demonstratest that thy knowledge of thyself is the knowledge of God. And he who knows himself is other than God; then how can other than God know God, and how can it be united to Him?—

Then the Answer is: He who knows himself understands that his existence is not his own existence, but his existence is the existence of God, without his existence becoming the existence of God (whose name be exalted) and without his existence entering into God or proceeding forth from Him, or his existence being along with Him or in Him. But he sees his existence in the condition in which it was before it was at all. So there is no extinction nor effacement nor extinction of extinction. For the extinction of a thing presupposes its independent existence first, and its independent existence presupposes its subsisting by itself, not by the power of God (whose name be exalted)—which is clearly absurd.

Understand, therefore, that the knower's knowledge of himself is God's knowledge of Himself, because his soul is nothing but He. And the Prophet (upon whom be peace) meant by the 'soul' the existence. And whoever attains to this state, his existence is no more, outwardly or inwardly, aught but the existence of Him (whose name be exalted). Nay, his existence is the existence of God (whose name be exalted), and his word the word of God

20

(whose name be exalted), and his act the act of God, and his claim to the knowledge of God is a claim to the knowledge of himself. But thou hearest the claim as from him, and seest the act as from him, and thou seest his existence to be other than God, as thou seest thyself to be other than God, by reason of thine ignorance of the knowledge of thyself. Then if "the believer be the mirror of the Believed,"[16] he is He, in His own eye, that is, in His own sight, for his eye is the eye of God and his sight is the sight of God. And he is not He in thine eye, or thy knowledge, or thy understanding, or thy imagination, or thy thought, or thy vision. But he is He in His eye and His knowledge and His vision. So if one say "I am God," then hearken to him, for it is God (whose name be exalted) saying "I am God," not he. But thou hast not attained to that to which he has attained; for if thou hadst attained to that to which he has attained, thou wouldest understand what he says, and say what he says, and see what he sees.

And, generally, the existence of things is His existence, without their existing at all. But do not fall into an ambiguity by imagining from these demonstrations that God is created. For one of 'those who know' has said, "The Sufi is uncreated"; and that is after the perfect unveiling and the cessation of doubts and imaginings. But this saying (luqmah) is only for him who has a nature wider than

[16] A saying attributed to the Prophet.

21

the two worlds,[17] and as for him whose nature is like that of the two worlds, it does not concern him, for it is nobler than the two worlds.

And, universally, thou mayest understand that seer and seen, and Creator and created, and knower and known, and perceiver and perceived are one. He sees his existence in His existence, and knows his existence by His existence, and perceives his existence by His existence, without any quality of the perception and seeing and knowing and without the form itself of the perception and seeing and knowing existing.[18] It is as if his existence were without quality, and his seeing himself without quality, and his perceiving himself without quality, and his knowing himself without quality.

Then if one ask and say: In what light regardest thou all the hateful and loveable things? For if thou seest, for instance, refuse or carrion, thou sayest it is God (whose name be exalted),—

Then the Answer is: God forbid that He should be any such thing! But our discourse is with him who does not see the carrion to be carrion, nor the refuse as refuse. Nay, our discourse is with him who has sight and is not born blind. For he who does not know himself is blind and cannot see. And until the

---

[17] Material and immaterial.

[18] الادراك والرؤية والمعرفة (سورة or صورة حروف وجود بلا .

blindness depart he will not attain to these spiritual matters. But this discourse is with God, not with other than God and not with the blind. For he who attains to this station knows that he is not other than God. And our discourse is with him who has resolution and energy in seeking to know himself in order to know God, and who keeps fresh in his heart the image of his seeking and his longing for union with God; and not with him who has neither aim nor end.

Then if one ask and say: God (whose name be exalted) has said, "The eyes do not perceive Him, but He perceives the eyes."[19] But thou sayest the contrary of that. Therefore, what thou sayest is not true,—

Then the Answer is: All that we are saying is the sense of the expression "The eyes do not perceive Him," that is, there is no one, and no one has sight, able to perceive Him. Then if we suppose that there is another than He in existence, we must allow that that other perceives Him. But God (whose name be exalted) has warned us in His saying "The eyes do not perceive Him" that there is no other beside Him; meaning, no other perceives Him, but He who perceives Him is God (whose name be exalted). So there is no other except Him. He it is who perceives His own essence, not another. So "the eyes do not

[19] Koran, VI, 103.

perceive Him," simply because the eyes are nothing but His own existence. And if anyone say, "The eyes do not perceive Him, only because they are of recent origin, and what is recent does not perceive what is old and permanent," he does not yet know himself, since there is nothing and there are no eyes except Him. He, then, perceives His own existence, without the existence of the perception and without quality.

Hymn

I know the Lord by the Lord, without doubt or
    wavering.
My essence is His essence in truth, without defect or
    flaw.
There is no becoming between these two, and my
    soul it is which manifests that secret.
And since I know myself without blending or
    mixture,
I attained to union with my Beloved, without far or
    near.
I obtained gifts of the Lord of Affluence without
    upbraiding and without recrimination.
I did not lose to Him my soul, nor does it remain to
    the lord of dissolution.

Then if one ask and say: Thou positest God and deniest the existence of aught else. What, then, are these things which we see?—

Then the Answer is: These discourses are with him who does not see aught beside God. And he who sees aught beside God (whose name be exalted), we have no question and answer with him, for he does not see other than what he sees. And he who knows himself does not see other than God, and he who does not know himself has not seen God; and every vessel exudes that which is in it. And we have explained much above, and if we should explain more than that, he who does not see would not see, nor understand, nor perceive; and he who sees, sees and understands and perceives already; and "a sign is sufficient to him who attains." And as for him who has not attained, he would not attain by teaching *(ta'lim)*, nor instruction, nor by reiteration, nor by learning, nor by intellect; but only by the attraction of a shaikh who has attained and an intelligent instructor, travelling on the Path, being guided by his light, and walking in his strength, and so attaining to the end, if it be the will of God (whose name be exalted).

May God (whose name be exalted) grant success to us and you in all that He desires and loves, of word and deed, and theory and practice, and light and guidance. Verily, He is over all things powerful and fit to Answer.